BESHREW

ALSO BY DANIELLE PAFUNDA

Pretty Young Thing (Soft Skull Press, 2005)
My Zorba (Bloof Books, 2008)
Iatrogenic: Their Testimonies (Noemi Press, 2010)
Manhater (DUSIE, 2012)
Natural History Rape Museum (Bloof Books, 2013)
The Dead Girls Speak in Unison (Bloof Books, 2017)
The Book of Scab (Richochet Editions, 2018)

BESHREW

DANIELLE PAFUNDA

Poems from the manuscript appear in *Los hijos de Whitman Francisco Larios* editor & translator (Valparaiso 2017), *Hick Poetics* (an anthology of contemporary rural American poetry) Abraham Smith & Shelly Taylor editors (Lost Roads Press 2015), *Academy of American Poets Poem-a-Day, Colorado Review, Denver Quarterly, The Equalizer, and Ping-Pong the Official Literary Journal of the Henry Miller Library.*

The line 'Beamy the world, yet a blank all the same' is borrowed from Robert Browning.

Layout and Book Design: DUSIE
dusie.org | Rhode Island

First printing, 2019.

ISBN-13: 978-1-944253-05-9
ISBN-10: 1-944253-05-X

Library of Congress Number: 2018943573

Beshrew that heart
that makes my heart
to groan!

William Shakespeare
Sonnet 133

I call to report the body. Call the number carefully
copied out on a newspaper margin,

my husband's desk. The body, I say,
is out there in the marsh. The body

has clothes on, shoes. It's been shot.
There's been a shooting. And hang up.

I delete the number and fisted-sleeve
wipe the screen, the looking-glass

where every secret sucks air and drowns
in data points. I suck air.

When I call to report the body, I do so
from my husband's desk. His files

hum to themselves in deep dream. I report
the body in my own voice, on my own time.

It isn't every hour one's heart gags. Just some.

What is the angle of impact? What
is the point of origin? At what

height did the butcher stand and what
breadth his wings when spread? What

word was lisped into blood spatter? What
rat did the body come to rest? What

whinges there beneath the wharf?
Whose tangled red silk lining? What

should we tell the papers? In what
solution was the jaw dissolved? What

killed which part of the body first? What
were they doing out alone at that hour?

Whatever it was, it can't be good. Whatever the
children saw from barges and trashcans whatever

the banshee wailed—over whose roof we don't know.

My husband's herringbone tie.
My husband's pinstriped jacket.

My husband's hat size, the band.
My husband's rosewood valet.

My husband's footfall on the drive. My husband's
agile fingers in my culvert, remembered.

My husband's leather soles stained and peeling
from an unexpected slog in the marsh.

My husband taken by surprise.
My husband reeling backward.

My husband after the shotgun blast
but before the long-houred drive.

My husband's woolen muffler. My husband's
match gone smolder. My husband's kiss goodnight.

My husband's broken hem, the hanger.

There's a rust stain on the porcelain
where my heart pounded. Tender

copper-tasting thread the tongue rounds.
Arch deep into that throat-rooted muscle.

I'm a carbon slug swaddled in sour sheets.
What time of day is it? I don't go in to work

anymore, I don't go get the children from school.
This blinking faucet of regret compounds me.

I am every drop plus its last, its echo, and
its mineral trace scumming the drain.

Who filled a bag with flies and burst it over
the heads of a thousand schoolgirls?

Who dug a pit ten-feet deep and filled it
one-foot deep with insects, some of whom

each other, and some of whom the guest?

I'm feeding your pages into the storm drain.
My hands covered in the broken bodies

in gutter crud, failed refuse. Twigs
catch a page so annotated it's scabbed.

My nightgown catches the curb. Headlights
wash my back, a surprise each time

to possum hunched over her bad brood.
Until up pulls my husband.

He stills the car. The wind goes still.
The headlights scald or scold me.

I drop the book. Stupid. It'll travel
below our house, across the border.

My arms ask, are you happy now? And
when he exits the vehicle, and when he guides

my elbow in his glove so soft it is in fact his hand.

As a feral thing would. As a dead leaf
whose crunch she herself hears, whose

buggy interior floods the sidewalk. *Beamy*
the world, yet a blank all the same.

Where you've tucked your pen into your notes,
I tuck my fingernail, burned and cursed and

shut tight my eyes. I tuck my feet up like a girl.
In this corner, warm milk fall of light something

far from revealing its milk-corpse eyes, that is,
the eyes downcast in every portrait, shaded

the ribbon a bright blue furl across the gaze, the
peculiar mother, her arm around a naked toddler

the fall of light. Betrays nothing. The book in
hand, betrays. As a feral thing would, I shred its

binding and burn through it for warmth.

Come alone for just as long as we need
to exchange hostages and a grease fire.

Eyes igniting every stitch of reticence,
every decent posture you are so inclined

are so good, I will make sure you can't
find this book. I will burn this book

every time you pick it up. This book
is catching fire imagining your hand

on its bare spine. My spine is catching fire
I drop to the ground's deepest curvature.

You cannot keep ahead of this.
Each pulse does as much damage

as the hard frequency of cells mismatched
allows. I have something of yours.

In the afterdeath of perfection, wait there.

I attend a genetically modified sonata.
My heart leaps, a stag into the copse.

A hart into the pool. Its deep end
awkward. A dashed bat on its surface

wings spread with dim web collecting
night bugs, weak signals. I dive into

the pool, something amiss. A cloud
of blood, a spilled chemical, the rise

and fall of strings. I spare you but not
the detail. I wipe my eyes clean

no longer alone on the tile. A set
of muscles fans and leaps beneath you.

I prepare myself a place you enter
and resign myself an exit. Stupid

brief halt of breath, stupid sweet thunder.

I eat foam and worms directly from your mouth.
I shiver in a neck brace while you count the

winnings. I nestle down into your hovel as you
write. I nestle into your past. If the things you

write aren't real. When they put us on trial for
obstruction of good feeling, will you hold my

hand? Will you firmly between my legs and secure
me? Will you pivot as though I exhibit to the jury,

so that I am pulse evidence? There's a question
you'll have to answer. Where were you the night

I was found bleeding from the mouth, vomiting
into the street from the open door of a rolling

Cadillac? Where were you the night I took my life,
stripped it from my skull like a face? And bagged

it tightly. Where were you when I ran for the train?

I can't stop. Stored up until loosed one after the
other, I jag them out for you. I touch every page

palm flat heaven's skull shuddering. The imprint, a
rubbing. My tongue lit with some narcotic phrase

come from the past-dead pleasure camp, come
gunning from some other moon, from pleasure's

own splitting fabric. I tour you from this unsafe
distance. Through the page I travel back to the page's

inception. I enter your hand hovering, your hot face
where something bolts in the dark and your dark

chest arcing with jumpstart. There's a tether in your
teeth, wire reverb to each wrist. All the rampant

forgiveness. You think the story will forgive.
Everyone forgives the hate, the whale's grief, the

white panic ruining the shoreline.

Where will I touch you, my hand under the dais
when we report on the intelligence failure?

Where, like a dream in which the affect
suddenly balloons and warps, will I hinge

our two bodies? Were there anything comely
in this painscape, I'd strip it for you.

I'd give it a thin coat of lace and through
some cocktail long out of fashion drag

each mink note of your voice in argument.
Answer his question. Then.

That man? In the audience? Answer
his meaningless question

while we all die here at various speeds
and justice establishes its next wound

that wet reticule your mouth, my every.

Rarely. I don't think of your pleasure
very often for fear of stepping into traffic

into shatter glass, into a revelation I cannot
buy myself back from. I think of your thigh

and every trade becomes contraband. Your
bare arm a thousand degrees pinned between

my legs. Your bare shoulder nailing my neck.
I convulse on the sheet, on the concrete

expanse of this loft floor, where am I?
Every city I go to reeks of you. Every

block, every hot black gust of right now.
When the lights go out, I press down

against insect wings and seraphimic grit.
Baby teeth, scavengers, thousands.

You cut me here. I suit you.

You arrange the eclipse to direct me
across the hotel bar. You arrange

for these rectangular suits to watch me.
I have a playing card where my wink

used to be. I make a blindfold of rat's skin. I jam
dough deep in my ears. Do what you want, now.

I pull a trash bag up to my neck and lace tight
its red bands. I cover my face in a thick layer

of honey and egg whites. I recite a rhyme,
I punish myself for reciting a rhyme.

In a puddle of melting ice. Pour a bottle of gin
over the body. Pour a bottle of turpentine

over my heavily made-up face. This face isn't
mine, it's the face I wear when I go looking for you

and I want you to think I'm home, a good woman.

I can't publish this. It's all about your raw
purchase on me. It's your raw mouth raw

against my bare-faced disaster every ticking
hellscape deteriorating until the rich fucking

wealth of hate, malice, government, law,
the sovereign citizen, dread, wretched power

recombines this particular fetish for your
scent. I can't publish this because everyone

can identify you by the passage over which
I cream my heart out. Everyone can see me

repeatedly creaming into the future. Your name
in my rigorously laced-up cache.

My wet, red, clairvoyant longing answers
all the equations with your DNA, your fingerprints

stretched out and restrung with pearls, my horse.

The guilt keeps my hand coiled tightly
jammed deep into this text, sweating,

loosening letter from language until I'm
a mess of ohhhhhhh, a glistening salvage

pounding out of the harbor, a wreck
of ropes and buckling hot metal frame.

I drown you repeatedly, scrabble over your body.
Your body, your mind/body split, your thinking

in terms that cream me into the next century.
I faint repeatedly into my own splayed arms.

Everything more than once, infinitely resistant
when you detail the disappearance of mothers

from their infants' mouths and still all I want to do
is cram your face with my batshit scatter. All I do

is stutter and hail against the thought of you.

I want something bad to happen. So badly.
Crush all the sweet furred feelings against the roof

of your dove-wrung mouth. Give my pulsing
regalia a hook to hang from. Or rope me, or burn

me. Or in the gutterheat morning look so ashamed
we both. It's a vengeful fuck rained down. My.

I hold it out to you. My. I arch it lashed to the
bedpost.All your young fans go red around the

ears, all the old stallions with their hot breath in
the cold night, but I am sterile as a nurse's brow.

Until you come stranglebound into every minute,
gulping hard through the ribs, demanding

one word after another until you've filled
the margin. Exposed the verbs all wet with effort.

The indecent margin of our failure.

I tail my lover to her workshop
where she compounds her own charcoal.

Vegetable scraps litter the floor. A fire
reduces, hinges gray crackle to fiber.

Her braid's been caked with mud and hay
to keep it pure. Did you know about her?

It's bright down here, not like you'd think,
her downy arms, my bruised up feet.

Where've you been? she wants to know.
At the harbor. Nowhere, nothing, never, I'm fine.

Her salvia seedlings, a tray of embryos, some kind
of mushroom. I cross my legs where a page of

your book threatens to drip out. I suck gloomily,
roll over, and regard my lover's work.

Nothing's live or dead no more. Just like that, it's so.

As a horse would. A wild horse would.
Mane whipping, no saddle, buck until

dragged, as from the lake's bottom, in the dead
of winter you come gasping back to life.

How does it feel to know
you will walk this world forever

in the same stupid body
that even now forbids you pleasure?

In the dark, my bit flashing, whites rolling
I have a thunder of misgivings. Give me

your rope to thread through my connective tissue.
Dump all this foul wine down my flank

and flush the snow from my cheeks.
I have never felt so alone as when

your book sunk down deep in the river I tossed it.

Butcher's jaw that I imagine cracking cold wind.
Your hands gloved and poured into fists, your

forearms bare, slit and peppered with diamond grit.
With the blood that spills from diamond

mines, with the blood that spills from very bad
children, with me. I sit still in my skin hating my

borders. Give me another way to hear your voice.
Give me a recording detailing the contents of a

genocide. You're bored, now, by my insistence on
horror. I hold up a man's skull, shattered on one

side, a piece of his skin still clings to it. Everything
mirror-imaged, terror-imaged, strung-out junkified,

ripped through the heart with politics. I don't want
you to think this has anything to do with you.

It has nothing.

Get the fuck away from me, then. I'm sick and free.
I've puked out my heart and also my organs.

My liver spills, my kidneys spill, my blood turns
the color of a nuclear sunset and hums across

the spoiled garden path. I've been at these stones
with the deadblow. I've been nailing the doors shut.

At sunset, I drowned your book in the river.
At the river, two large men grabbed my arms.

They pinned me against a shipping container.
They tore your words from my throat and held them

in the pink arc cast by a security light. *Give him up*
they told me, and I did. Over and over again

retching into their outstretched sack, retching
money and grief and the look of your hair

plastered down by an oily rain.

Don't think you know me. First of all, I'll never
let you see this book. Second of all, you don't.

I'm stranded in your grief and sweat. When you
buried your father, I lay myself deep in his grave.

When your sister's heart burst, I lay myself down
on her gurney and swore through the gaping vale.

And swore. And swore. Your pennies, ragged pens,
ragged love and lovers ground their teeth to ash,

their desperate finances, their cow-eyed sleeper eyes,
all lash. What's to tell? I'm immensely patient.

When we go to the governor's mansion to sing
an ode to state, I wear your mother's perfume

and your dog's collar. So you cannot bear to snap
the leash and you cannot stop calling me to heel?

We have no ethical content.

With my side of the bed cum-dulled.
With a bucketful of pebbles to load your pockets.

With wet coffee grinds for your pockets.
With dead songbirds circling the base of the tree.

With a blood soaked gag in your pocket.
With an impossible trail of breadcrumbs down to

the riverfront. With no phone in my pocket.
With a shadow felled over the scene.

With your silhouette disappearing around the
corner. With a rat eating its way into my pocket.

With nowhere to duck, no niche, no pocket.
With the side of my face cum-dulled.

With my hand against the roof of the car, an air-
pocket. With your voice in my ear a leftover high.

From whose dreary pocket did tweeze the name?

My lover gets hold of this book and won't
stop. *Is he alive or dead? she asks, alive or dead?*

Is it him? Yes, I say, no, who cares. My discreet
husband gets wind of it. My lover, she knows.

The mechanic I'm fucking, the mothers in the
schoolyard. *Are you sad, Mama,* the children ask,

are you singing? Everyone knows such keening
is mine. A silver net of frost covers my face, hands

sliced clean from my body. I might be eighteen in
the dirt circle, again, the maiden betrayed by Papa.

Sold for a penny, sold for a pound. *Who are you,*
I ask the mice. *Who are you* they build nests among

frozen limbs. My birthday. Time to go the bell rings
I assume thaw. Your name bleeds slowly

through my blouse, a vole carved it thus.

Time to touch touch touch you. Time to spell it
out. Letter by primly snipped letter from your

book. My fingers bleed, letters stick. Time to
touch you is all the time in the world is bed

enough and time. Get me the sheets, get me
wrapped in a winding sheet and drug, dragged

out the back door at daybreak. There's a letter
in my husband's pocket. A letter of letters clipped

for ransom. For a thousand dollars and a bag of
dope and a couple of tickets to the boxing match

held in a freighter on the tracks. I'm dragged at
dawn, out the door the sheet conforms, sun

water pours. A fleeting sensation of heat suck and
oxygen deprivation. I lie in the yard, twisting,

arrived the moment the plan must be executed.

Did I embarrass you, petting on you like that?
On the trading floor I corner you and rub your

chest with my bidding paddle. *Fifty*! I holler. *One-*
fifty! I holler. I ask you to sign it, to sign your book

in tongue. Or blood. Anything you have on you.
I promised them I wouldn't read your book again.

Look what I wrote up my legs and across my
stomach— My thighs are shaking with it.

I can't stand up. Every word is your finger, heated
iron into deep tissue. What would it take to get

you to run your finger over one of your own
phrases copied out in my hand, breaking skin in

places running my stockings, running my breath
up the limb where it freezes, a cat in prowl gone

too far? What would it take to coax me down?

I like trouble more than sex,
so this is what you catch me making.

You catch me vomiting up a hasty
pair of trousers. A shoelace dangles

from my lip. I close my mouth,
skinny streak of leather everything

you need to know. Tonight.
Tomorrow you'll deny it.

My face on a touchscreen backlit
by your heavily crafted redactions.

One fat, wet slash after another. No
scrawl, sentimental scuzz, betrayal

of heart by hand. Not you. That shadow
you stretch across my mouth, that regal

band of nevermore I chew through after all.

Be sure, I had a best friend when I met you.
I was chock full of dirty rats, supper club tables,

tumbling superstars, glasses shattered.
I cried hotly well through my thirties.

I had a ring of familiars. Who were you
to glisten so hard, bawling?

Bailing out my well? Slugging
a salty kapow, your shirt turned inside-

inside? Inside the cuff of your jacket
where they stitch a spare brass button.

I stitched the spent muscle
that was my tongue, a gem

from the spit-valve, your dopey
rhythm gone stuffing its wet snout

into the business of life and death and sex again.

On your chest are printed the names of the dead.
Each one, the same as all others, rents you.

Stand naked in the hall, the night air
and something crosses vandalous.

Your grave sings. Opens wide and rips a string
from its own throat. Oh fresh expanse of

pleasure-proof male body, I gape toward you
myself all throne-rag. The discreet droplet

in my lung, one of affection's tragedite fossils.
Unrelieved, gasp in nests of pearls and fiberglass.

Hair, muscle and flesh. The ink in the needle smug
as it slips under your skin. What I cannot do is press

my fingers into the equator that divides your body
from flight and longing. I cannot press

my skin well enough to yours to transfer.

I set your copyright page on fire. I light it and
set it in my own hand and my own hand burns.

I drop it into my lap and it catches fire again. I
drop. I drop down, drops of something sticky on

the tiles. It's dripping from me. I drain my heart
and watch it pool, gambol, run sour into the ash.

I take you out of the library of congress. I take you
out of congress and you come wheeling into

perfection with each break. I break into each word.
I break each word between my teeth, mouth full of

paper, and letters drooling down my chin. I'm
sobbing mascara over the paper, new words leaking

into the gut of the book. But there's nothing new
about [redactions]

or gasoline in which they hold my head under.

This is how I get you to come in the yard. I set
the bees loose. I set the dogs loose. I sting the

horses and set them loose, their eyes showing
white. I shoot daggers. I fill the garden with

daggers. I slip a dagger into the mailbox. I slip on
a dagger and every flagstone trembles beneath me.

Perched on the fence in lace cuffs, I cough, I take
blood from my lips with lace.

I lace my ankles together. I'm bound at the knees.
My thighs are soaked. I'm lost at the knees. I'm

bound by the throat. I'm trussed to the fence. I'm
wet from the pond. I'm wept from the pond. I

wash up the mud coming streak by streak off my
skin in the light of one half-dead moon and

do not prefer any reader over myself.

Ratty, Ratty, boom-ba-latty
how does your garden grow?

I want you to see me and convulse. Whatever you
were that loved me is dead now. In your heart a thread

has caught, a tooth, my hair, a nail from which they
can sever my code and convict us both. Don't call the

candle catching on my slip, my slip the wet tile, the
pool of water so hot for oxygen and affection. I want

you drowning over and over again in my bathtub, my
arches pressed into the porcelain, the tile sweating

regret. The phone rings out of the past. The squad car
arrives with its black and white flair. Its list of words

that break me. I give up everything before they even
ask. I hold everything out, hold out, my fingers laced

with shallow cuts my hands red for you where I traced
your margin over and over again. Where I placed my

lip. Where I couldn't breathe but breathe you in.

I bleach long thin strips of paper from your
book and hush

Then I eat the paper, nearly severed, soggy
dripping and spoiled. Such soft quiet eating

in the soft quiet light! Night done
running its cord through my lungs.

The table heaves in charcoal and silk scrap
and hush

Rather, air, dust, and sunshine negotiate
whatever's in my ribcage, gagged.

I eat your dull blankfaced book. I bleach
my throat clean, my gut, my stony cold.

And then I bleach my starry eyes.
It's like a wedding gown in here,

lavishly nothing left to sell. And.

When they knife you in the gut, it's my blood that
tumbles out. When they open the closet where

you've hanged yourself, again I tumble.There's no
moon tonight, and my hands are bound.

The dream gag, a handkerchief, gleams bright. My
head aches from the chloroform, from the coming

storm. The metal chair leaves a cold line.
In the other room, the crisp ring of a bullet in the

bottom of a highball glass. A couple of big guys
guard me, and one presses the phone to my mouth.

Tell him. So I do: *It's all or nothing. My house is on
fire. My baby's alone.* Then they gag me back up

and I go spinning down into the well where they keep
all the busted up lovers who used to love you.

Every last drop in the rusted cup.

In the shipping container, I begin an opera.
It stars what I'm sure is a rat and a scratching

sound in the corner behind me. It stars
the unmixed stink of ammonia and must.

I compose an aria for you by rearranging
the letters of your derelict promise.

I hum it over the gag that binds my tongue
and tastes of motor oil, salt, boiled peanuts

in cotton. I'm not interested in the bind.
I'm only interested in the gag. My clutch

on your name. My grunt slams into its
concentric stars. The Scratching halts.

You think I'm the victim in the scene?
There's a stiletto in my throat

that no one's thought to frisk for.

A rat is my ghost of choice tonight.
A rat comes shining through the garden gate.

He's got bulbs by the sackful, he's got
the debts of the dead in dripping paper sacks.

He sets a bag of mulch against the yew tree.
What cold plug are you screwing in there?

I wrench a wad of paper and ice from the birdbath.
Aye. Says the rat and punches my face.

Do you know the one about the missus
with a snakes' nest heart and stones for lovers?

I. I do. And plunge my fist back in the bath.
The rat whistles his way to the plum trees, just

sticks, just ten thin bones under the rock-hard moon.
And burlap shrouds unraveling their seams.

We're all widows tonight, so that rat dons his gowns.

I don’t want you to think this is about domesticity.
It’s a good thing I can’t feel or touch you. Your

mouth studded with sugar. I collapse you at the
end of a long hallway, peacock carpets, gilded

elevator doors. I’m not prepared to look after a
grown man. Walls in forest mural, and there you

crouch in every tree. A few minutes of every
day for the rest of my lifeache, I’m in love with

you. I’m sitting at the end of your bed wraithe-
scaped, my hair done up in a twist. Your hair

raked back with your fingers when you’re going
full throttle regret. But I don’t. Foxed crypt.

Epitaphs running. Running for your life
underground, wet tunnel, arms trembling

over your head. This is politics. This is it.

A rat brings me a bottle of Xanax.
Drink up now, love, hair on your chest.

My therapist from the cold place
comes in wearing her name tag.

A flock lifts up, spring water cracks,
her heels shifting on the metal floor.

In this visit, the shipping container is bare.
We will address my inability to stay present

in the moment. She scrapes up dust,
rat droppings, cigarette butts

and showers them over my head.
She asks me to write my name

with my tongue on a mirror she holds
a few inches from my face. I reach—

I fail and reach deep back into time.
There are many people dead on the inside

who'd like to cum on my face, my husband tells me.

Going down on the dead sisters in a metal box
will change your life. They hold hands.

They smell like jasmine, milk, and cryptal clemency.
Full-throated. They'll screw your

thumbs to the bed post gates. This is the waiting
room, the operating room. This is the drawing

and quartering room. The game room. This is the
room in which none of your questions will be

answered. Justice, hopped up on dex and treasure,
muses fleshly-corseted, freshly-ledged, leaning

over precariously. Their hair brushes your face.
So what's new? What's in the bag they hold?

You've been up for three nights, wringing your
bound hands in a rusted rectangle. Your own DNA.

You think any politico ever got here by chance?

I vain crush
against your windpipe.

I am close
coming close

dragging down your neck
rope wrapped & bucking.

Nothing splintered,
nothing gained. Splayed

as ever all our boring-oring-oring limbs
the sign of true affection. Boo hoo.

You leave wife after wife
at the bottom of the well.

The sleeper has a fist.
He curls it 'round his fat coin.

Just for me, don't you?

Rat and Skinny went to bed.
Rat rolled over and Skinny was dead.

In the shipping container, unearned terror is
rubbed over my skin with a raw rag, the grodiest,

that bound mouths cracked, mouths bleeding
and saliva-caked, foam-speckled or given up.

People whose deaths actually mattered, or
something. Every vision I have = incredibly stupid.

My heart pukes itself in my throat. I gurgle
a mouthful of vomit and abiding affection. You

are the sum total of words I remember. The tune.
I gush your book from a crack in my lip.

I recite it through the gag. I'll never get ransomed.
No. No ransom frees a bitch so far gone.

Oh lonesome girls who won't turn out the light.
Won't you ride me home? Won't you wear this rag,

a flag to burn in the dirt lot behind the grocery?

This is the book in which I love you. This is Option 1.
I cannot bear thinking about you when you are

nowhere near to hand so I shove you off this pier
with my face set to zero. This is Option 2 by the

millisecond you create the setting for this evacuation
of reason. In Option 3, you take me to a room for

fucking my brains out. You lock me up with you in
the shipping container. That container which allows

for no dawn but a crack of sick light oozing through
its metal tinder. Also you love me. You love me back

as though whenever you read the poem you wrote for
me, you will speak my name and meet my eye.

What was it like? Memory fries and fakes a heartache.
Wails out of me a tinny pop song in my pockets.

Rabid, were the page a valid future.

Today you can adore me.
You can pull a soiled rag

from your pocket & shove it
deep in my throat & on it

I'll taste all the other women
you've gagged, the people

of color, the Jews, the queers,
the itty-bitty babies.

I'll taste how much love
goes into the securing of limbs

against the bedpost of a narrative
you're puking out in a very

warm cavern, deep under
the shipyard, deep under

my stationary hull.

I don't wonder what they're thinking
while lightly choking me creaming

my chest biting slapping me
against the wall. My lover,

some lover. My husband. The pills
are lined up on my bound wrists, my

stacked wrists, and I tongue each one
carefully into my mouth. A board

has been placed across the arms
of this chair. My arms rest there a judgment.

They're thinking what we all grunt
and think with a heave. What time is it?

The crack grows dark and something chitters
near the base of the shipping container. My legs

numb, tilt into sleep first, and I race after them.

A bundle of clawed insects
had come untied in my lap.

I wished I were dead, but I have
all these children. You know

what they say about dead mothers.
When crying over you

in a hot shower became
too tender a luxury.

When wrapping a thick towel
around my head while my husband

birthed obscenities became
too plush a hobby, I thought I'd go.

Now, my chain stretches two feet,
and I circle my chair, a raw ankle

to pivot, but I don't feel any better.

It's gritty on this loose slab of Lino.
A millipede waves its feet.

It's romantic and prehistoric.
I used to live in places like this

because I didn't have money
or charm. When I got tired

of repacking my bag. When I
wanted to play a kind of squashed hat

grizzled beard, was made before I was born
for a woman with even less promise

with even fewer plans to roll
out of the storm drain into the road

last century's roadkill.

Whose wet foot on the floor? Surely
not the body's. Whose wet prints damaging

the wood the wool the wool pulled over?
Whose nightgown strangling whose thighs?

Whose hair in silent wet chains wrapping
whose neck a modernist shade, no pulse

as she sweeps up the stairs? Whose finger
slippery on the screen as she punches in

the passcode, the number one has even
in death tattooed on her tongue,

the number for which one bit her tongue
nearly in half and like Philomel

scratched it with her hell-hot breath
into the side of a rusted hold? Beshrew,

she scrawled and carved the heart.

DANIELLE PAFUNDA is the author of eight books including *The Dead Girls Speak in Unison* (Bloof Books), *Natural History Rape Museum* (Bloof Books), *Manhater* (DUSIE) and the speculative memoir, *The Book of Scab* (Ricochet Editions).

SIE

DU

www.ingramcontent.com/pod-product-compliance
Ingram Content Group UK Ltd.
Pitfield, Milton Keynes, MK11 3LW, UK
UKHW041842200726
13854UKWH00005BA/1993
9 781944 253059